CYNTHOLOGY

A **COLLECTION** OF **RHYMES**

CYNTHIA YOUNG

AuthorHouse™ LLC
1663 Liberty Drive
Bloomington, IN 47403
www.authorhouse.com
Phone: 1-800-839-8640

Published by AuthorHouse 05/09/2014

ISBN: 978-1-4969-0536-9 (sc)
ISBN: 978-1-4969-0537-6 (e)

Library of Congress Control Number: 2014907032

First paperback edition May 2014

For information about special discounts for bulk purchases, please contact
Cynthia Young, at 1-951-205-9810 or cyoungbooks@gmail.com

Available in E-Book and Soft Copy at www.authorhouse.com

Cover design by www.shutterstock.com

Contents

Introduction

Cynthology is a collection of unedited rhymes that express my view of life. Drawing from my grief, I wrote my first poem in 2007 as a way to express my feelings about my youngest aunt, who passed away that year. After that, rhymes became a means of expression that I continue to use.

My friends asked me how I came up with these rhymes—I was inspired from things they said or did; something I heard on the television or something that just came to mind.

Sometimes, there is no rhyme or reason to the things that happen in life. Good and bad experiences are inevitable, there will be peaks and valleys, triumphs and tragedy, laughter and tears during our lifetime.

I covered a variety of subjects; whether it was a current issue or something from the past. The rhymes seemed to tell a story, so I describe them as short stories that rhyme.

It is my pleasure to give you straight talk, gut wrenching, comical and sensual stories to entertain you. Enjoy!

Cynthia Young

Dedicated to those that stood with me in the past, stand with me now and look forward with me to the future

Cynthology

Cynthia Young
October 21, 2013

Cynthology is my view of life
From being a kid in a good neighborhood
To becoming a wife

Life is good, bad or indifferent
I've been to the school of
Hard knocks and bumps
Believe me, I've
Paid my dues and handled my lumps

Love, happiness, loved ones loss
I dealt with many until
They went home to the big Boss

I have good friends, known many men
And stuck with the good one
That put a ring on it in the end

Now it's my time to shine
Drink some wine and dine
Drive the rode and see what
I dream about

I'm finally free to be me and I want to
Shout it out!

Struggles

Cynthia Young
August 02, 2012

Struggling day by day
Trying to figure out a way
To survive
Makes you drop to your knees
Begging the Lord, please oh, please
Prayer changes things, yes it does
Keep your head up and look to the sky

But, resentment and anger
Creep in each time
You take another blow to the chin

The rent is due, the lights are off
Can't make that car note
And
I got beef with my boss

I have to turn it around, but how?
My baby tells me
To turn my frown upside down

Things will be alright, I believe it
With all of my might
Lotto winnings are yet another dream
I have at night

One day my ship will come in
Because the Lord will put up His hand
And
Deflect those blows from my chin

Detroit

Cynthia Young
June 05, 2012

Detroit, I love your
Motown sound

I was a kid in the 60's when I heard
The Temptations,
Marvin Gaye and the Four Tops
For the first time

Mustangs, Cadillac's, Electra 225
The big three auto makers
Pumped out the coolest rides

Belle Isle and the Bob Lo Boat
Bring lots of good memories
To mind

We danced at the Greystone
And
The 20 Grand
Listening to all our favorite bands

Lions and Tigers, cheered on by fans
Big D baseball caps
Can be seen on most any man

Through riots and fires
You still struggle for life
Neighborhoods tell a sad story of strife

My home town still has plenty of pride
Stand up big D
And
Come back to life!

The Fabric of My Life

Cynthia Young
May 28, 2012

Memories flood my mind
Thinking of all the family and
Friends that have been left behind

They're not gone, I have
Woven them like thread through
My mind

You may remain
Or you have
Come and gone, but you
Make up the Fabric of My Life
Like a
Beautiful song

I am who I am because you
Passed my way
If just
For a moment, month, year or day

Many people have come my way
Bringing heartache, anger, love
Happiness, their wisdom and joy

They exposed and encouraged me to
Experience what was on the other
Side of life's unopened door

Just Be You

Cynthia Young
May 28, 2012

I do what I do
You do what you do
Don't worry about me
Just be you

You never have anything
Nice to say, always
A put down from you
Every day

You act like a hater
I see green in your eyes
Your jealousy and venom
Are hard to disguise

Don't try to be me
What's wrong with you!

You don't even like me
But you want to do
What I do

Love the skin <u>*you're*</u> in!
And
Stop pretending to be my friend

Leo

Cynthia Young
March 2007

We were Leo's sharing a lion's ferocity
From within our souls

You played with me, dressed me like a doll, plaited my
Hair and wiped ice cream from my face
You were my teacher helping me to survive in this human race

You were kind, fierce but gentle. I felt your love that I will
Continue to embrace and kindle

Loving life, laughter, music and fun you were sassy, sexy and always
Took your place in the sun

You were a strong woman coming from good stock, and often times
You were my rock

In '74 I left this Motor City but returned for many visits
Each time anxious to see you, to ask if
There was anything I could do

Then one day, the tables turned and it was time for me to be strong
And take my turn
It was clear to me you couldn't manage on your own
And now you are gone

The day you died, heaven opened up and cried
And
I came back to be by your side

So just know, as you journey through the sky,
I will miss you and I can not say goodbye
Because after a while,
I know we'll meet again on the other side

No Appreciation

Cynthia Young
May 15, 2012

When you help people out there is no
Doubt that the reward can be great
But, there are those that
Do not appreciate

It makes you think why would they
Try and bring
You down when you
Went out of your way

Then you get leery and sometimes
Real weary of helping anyone else

Friends are bad, but family can
Be the worse in lacking
Appreciation

Do this for me, do that for me
They always have out their hand
But when you need something
They act like they don't know
Your name

Jealousy is key you can bet on that
They know, I can always take care of me
They want to be slick
And
Play games and nasty tricks
And still don't have money
To get what they need

When they need you again, they come 'round acting like your friend
But wake up and see they don't appreciate you, or what you do
You're just somebody they can use

I Value You

Cynthia Young
May 13, 2012

I value you and everything
You do

You never miss your water
Until the well is dry
Oh, yes that's very true

I want you to know
While you're on this earth
Not when you go
That I value you

Nothing is better than having
You near, laughing, talking
And
Making sweet memories

These words are real
And
Express the way I feel
From my head to my heels
I value you

You have been here for me day after day
I won't ever take for granted
Your generous ways

There is no replacement for
The way you are
You'll always be in my heart
Whether you are near or far

Rise

Cynthia Young
May 20, 2012

You hated on me when I trusted you
You sided against me
When you thought there was
Something in it for you

You were greedy and
Because of your black heart
You'll always stay needy

You struck a low blow on me
Maybe doing that
Set you free

God don't like ugly
And
With Him on my side
I, will rise

I, will rise because
With you, I have been right
And
My prayers
Will give me
My might

I, will rise no matter
What you do
I'll get
Stronger and stronger
While hell will be waiting for you!

Crack Head

Cynthia Young
May 20, 2012

I'm a Crack Head, sleeping on the street
Trying not to wind up dead
Jittery and skittery, walking up and down
Looking for the next hit
All over town

I'm looking for a way out
Hope has died and I want it back
I don't know how, to get off
This Ferris Wheel

Right now, I'm just looking for
The next crack deal

Can help be far away
Will I ever get
To have my day?

I had aspirations and dreams too
Back in the day

I want what you have
But not in a bad way

Crack head
Is what people call me
Trust and believe
It's not the way I want to be, I need help

I promise you
I want to get off this dope
To be a better me and to stop
Being the butt of everyone's jokes

Will Work for Food

Cynthia Young
May 12, 2012

Always smiling, she's got lots of jokes
She stands by
My side, ready to help
Whatever the yoke

Picked her up one day
As
She stood on the curb
Holding a sign
Will Work for Food
When I saw that, I had no words!

My friend, Winnye
Always there,
Stepped to my car with
The wind in her hair

We laugh and we joke all through the day
But I listen
To her wise words
Whether we're at work or play

She's been
My fiercely loyal friend
All through the years

Will Work for Food
Is what the sign said
In return
I give her my friendship, loyalty and love
For the rest of my days

Cheater

Cynthia Young
May 10, 2012

Talking low on the telephone, acting like
You don't want to be at home

Making up excuses to leave
You just don't know
I'm on to your scheme

I get a funny feeling in my gut
And I know that you're playing
Around with some slut!

I can see the changes in you
How you treat me, ignore me
And keep me from you

You can't fool this woman's intuition
You can try all you want
But it's you, that your actions
Will come to haunt

Whatever you do is truly on you
Keep messing around
And
I won't be found

Because women like me, don't grow on vines
Somewhere out there, awaits a King that will see
All the value I have in me

So you go on **Cheater!**
And do what you do
And I won't even look
Back at you!

I'm a strong woman, yes I am!
And I won't take crap, from any man!

Cadillac Man

Cynthia Young
May 04, 2012

Cadillac's are fine as can be
There is nothing like it as far
As I can see

It's the smell of good leather and luxury
That makes my heart pump
And
It really pleases me

I bought one, but wanted two or three
Like Elvis, I'd have
A different one every day of the week

I love my Cadillac, yes I do
I'm riding with my top back
Picking up women across the track

I need to ride all over this town
And see how my Homie's are
Getting down

A 300 C, not for me,
I'm a Cadillac Man
And
Nothing else will do

Here I come to pick you up
To ride in Cadillac style

Playing my music, rocking my head
And
Riding along with a smile

Ego

Cynthia Young
April 29, 2012

Ahh, what can I say, Ego is everywhere
These days

The bigger it is the more
You walk blind through the maze

Egos tend to get in the way
Of love, happiness and friendships too

It's ruined many relationships
That otherwise would have
Survived, had not a big
Bad Ego come into your lives

Ego trips, can bring harsh words
To the lips
And once said to the
Universe, they are hard to reverse

Put that Ego in check
And
Stop making a mess, breaking hearts
And tripping all over yourself

Wake up and you'll see, Ego can't be
Bigger than me
I'm the one that has your back
Not your Ego, that's taken
Our relationship all off track

Ego is cool when used like a good tool
So be careful . . . .
Too much Ego, will make you look like a damn fool

The Schemer

Cynthia Young
April 29, 2012

A Schemer smiles, laughs and talks
Real slick, watch out because they
Have lots of tricks

A Schemer tells you what you
Want to hear and spends your
Money throughout the year

It's always something
You'll find out, with a
Schemer in your pocket
Day in and day out

Hard to tell sometimes who these
Schemers really are
From the outside or the inside
They could be riding in your car

Look for their anger when
They don't get their way
They'll circle around and
Hit you up another day

A Schemer is cavalier
Spending your money all
Over town

Next thing you know
Your coffers are down

A Schemer is certainly
The one going to frown
When you figure
Them out and shut
Their ass down

I Miss You

Cynthia Young
April 27, 2012

You've gone on your way and left
Me here, thinking about our yesterdays

My head knows that you had to go
But my heart still misses you so

The good times are what I'll have to
Remember, long after you've gone

Your tender touch that I love so much has
Burned in my skin and my soul

I see your face and hear your voice
When I close my eyes
I miss you and baby; that is no lie

All those memories will remain in
My head, like our sweet romantic songs

Take care of yourself and never forget
I'll get along one day at a time
But Honey, you'll always be on my mind

I'll be here waiting
Until I see you again
It's just a matter of time

Lip Service

Cynthia Young
April 17, 2012

We all know somebody that likes
To hear themselves talk
But never gets around to walking the walk

Big promises, big dreams
Never quite comes together it seems

They promise you the world
But never come through
Lip service is all they know how to do

They'll run their mouth and talk
Plenty of smack all while
Stabbing you in the back

Maybe one day, Lip Service will end and
Those big dreams, big promises
Will come at last

But don't count on it 'cause these people
Rarely get up off their ass and
Their promises never come to pass

Cynthia Young

Old Age Is a Bitch

Cynthia Young
April 15, 2012

Old age is a Bitch my momma once said
Now that I'm older I know what she means

Each morning I try to get out of bed
Aches and pains overwhelm me
Is this all in my head?

My mind is telling me I'm still young
Like I use to be
But my body knows the truth
And
It damn sure doesn't lie to me

So, I've got to get out of bed, get off my butt
And
Work through this aches and pains rut

Old Age is a Bitch, oh yes I see
I'll do whatever I can
To beat it back from me

I'll keep my eyes on the prize
And be the best I can be

'Cause Old Age is a Bitch
And
I pray those aches and pains
Won't keep a hold on me

Move Forward

Cynthia Young
April 14, 2012

Sometimes we just can't seem to move our feet
We're all bogged down and feeling beat!

We want to Move Forward
But can't give up the past
We can't see the future for
Looking back at what we did last

Move Forward and keep things fresh
Open your mind, your heart
And your eyes
New blessings will come
When you let go of the past!

Blood Doesn't Matter

Cynthia Young
April 14, 2012

Blood doesn't matter when there is a need
Friendship and love can be more binding than the seed

No matter, we didn't come from the same Mother
We have worked together like no other

Over the years we've washed each others tears
Shared each others fears, laughter and joy

It's true we've been through a lot
But there was never anything
We couldn't work out

I have your back and you have mine
Our friendship has grown with
Much love over time
And
Having you as my friend is
Divine

Blood doesn't matter when it comes to you
And
I know you feel
The same about me too

Nothing will separate us
Until it's time

"Friends 'til the end"
Is the last thing I'll say to
Close out this rhyme

Lost Love

Cynthia Young
April 09, 2012

Even though I wasn't with you a long time ago
Darling I really did love you so
My love never left you, please know

So young and so restless
I had to go
To pursue a dream I couldn't let go

I can't take it back, I wish I could
But those days of lost love
Are gone for good

I feel your resentment sometimes
It's something that you don't always hide

I pray you'll forgive me one of these days
For not being with you along the way

Don't let lost love keep us apart
I beg you, please let me into
Your heart

Now that you're grown, beautiful
And smart, maybe you'll let
Me see more of your heart

I'm here now and there's nothing
I won't do
To make up for the lost love
That always belonged just to you

A Different Time

Cynthia Young
April 09, 2012

A different time comes to mind
When I hear a song play on
The radio

It makes me sway, or bump and grind
Don't you know

Music transforms me to be
Anything I want to be
It puts pop in my hips and sweet
Words on my lips

Music makes me lean when I'm
Driving down the street
Listening to Marvin Gaye's
Soulful beat

I love the Motown sound it's
All around town, just look and
You'll see
Folks on the street corner
Getting down

A different time comes to mind
'Cause most of the songs
Playing today ain't worth
A dime

Down but Not Out

Cynthia Young
April 08, 2012

The economy sucks and it's hard
Making a buck

No jobs to get
Got a mortgage and bills to pay

I'm keeping my head up and
Looking to a brighter day

'Til then I'll take a deep breath
And hold up my chin

I might be down, but
I'm not out 'til the end!

No Prospects

Cynthia Young
April 07, 2012

Talking on the phone with my girl,
And she tells me, things aren't all that cool
In her world

Too many things not going her way
No money, no man, no prospects today

She says she's cool, 'cause the last thing
She needs, is some broke down tool

With no money, no job, no car and up to no good
Who wants to be with someone
Acting like a hood

She's content to be alone,
So there'll be no
Rejects up in her home

Instead of being with a dead head
There's something to be said,
About being alone in bed

Do what you got to do, use
Your toys to bring you joy

She swears, she's not worried and there's no hurry
No prospects now, doesn't **_mean_** . . . . She
Won't **eventually,** get the man of her dreams

High Heel Shoes

Cynthia Young
April 04, 2012

Now let me tell you about high heel shoes
You know how much they give our feet the blues

But, Baby you know how to strut your stuff
When you wear those sexy high heel shoes

There's no time to worry about corns on your feet
Show off your pretty legs as you sway down the street

Short skirts, pants and the like; don't have
Much flavor without that six inch spike!

So go on girl, give the high heel shoes a whirl
And rock your man's sexy world

There's no time to snooze 'cause he'll be peeping at you
While you slip out of your bad ass high heel shoes

He'll take off your clothes and slide down your hose
You'll love it when he's rubbing your feet
'Cause he ain't planning on letting you sleep

Dream to Reality

Cynthia Young
December 2013

I had a dream that looked like you and
The first time I saw you I knew it had come true

I loved your body, the way you walked
And talked

Dancing with you to our favorite song
Made me know loving you couldn't be wrong
My dream became reality through and through

My jealousy and insecurity ran you away
I knew you would leave me after I slapped you one day
I took you for granted and I was on the wild, never believing you
Really wanted to be my wife and have our child

I couldn't accept that you really loved me too
I lost my dream that became reality, but I will always
Remember how it felt to be loved by you and I
Pray you will remember some good things
About me too

Bootsie

Cynthia Young
January 22, 2012

Dedicated to Aunt Helen

Tough as nails, yet sassy and peppy
This bombshell loved her Pappy, she would fight tooth and
Nail to protect what was hers but
Never missed a chance to give someone kind words

Sisters and Brothers it really didn't matter
She was the one they turned to, to help fight a battle
But when she dressed up and strutted her stuff
You had to step
Back and not be in a huff

Right to the end she held up her chin
And sitting by her side was her niece
Pen-Pen

Bootsie and Mookie a dynamic duo
The last of eight
Was their planned fate

She leaves Mookie behind
But never fear
My Uncle awaits his Dear

Once again she will see her Love
And
Sleep peacefully with him among beautiful white doves

Let's Roll!

Cynthia Young
March 07, 2012

Dedicated to my friend and brother in law, Wallace

Hey Sis' Whuzz Up?

I had to work today and it was tough
I'm tired of the manager 'cause he ain't cool
He's getting on my nerves acting like a fool

But that's all good cause it's time to go
And I'm ready to roll don't you know

I'm going to put on my fur and head for the door
Just get yourself ready and you can go too
But make sure you put on those bad ass shoes

I say **Let's Roll!** to check on the golden girls
And see what's happening in their world

I look good in my Cadi riding along
With the sunroof open
Breeze blowin' and playing a song

It's all I ever wanted and it makes me feel special
'cause I worked hard to get to this level

Hold on to your memories of us as a team, taking care of
The GG's and never running out of steam

I'll see you around, so 'til then keep getting down
And you'll know I'm beside you when you roll into town

Now it's time for my last ride
Down the golden bricks to the other side

Let's Roll!
Will come to mind when you think of me
Just don't forget to smile
And remember, that "Gator"
Left this world,
In his White suit and Kangol hat
And went home in ultimate style

Caregiver's Elegy

Cynthia Young
March 2011
Excerpted from
"Memoirs of a Caregiver" by Cynthia Young

Dedicated to Caregivers everywhere

I pray that I will always care for those I love with passion and grace
But with all the caring comes responsibilities that are hard to face

These 24 hour days are some thing I don't
want, I'm not having any fun
I'm tired and it makes me sad
To see my loved one trying to hang on

I feel like screaming, shouting and crying out and
Some times it's hard to get my laughter out

I just want you back the way you were
Remembering the good times from back in the day
But this curve in the road has taken us a different way

No matter which way things go, you bring me joy
With your wise child like eyes and I know
That I'm really the one reaping the prize

When I see your smile and innocence now
There is only one thing for me to do
I just need to love, kiss and do all I can, to protect you

God has the master plan
And I know that Angels are guiding me through
To do what He has put me here to do

There is one thing that I can't overlook and that is to take care
Of myself, while I see to your needs
And follow God's plan where ever it leads

The Spoiler

Cynthia Young
April 29, 2012

Sitting around talking with my
Wife in Law
Wondering if one of us
Is going to get hit in the jaw

The Spoiler left home earlier today
His temper was off the
Hook and in a bad way

He's back, here he comes, he
Spoils all our fun
He just doesn't know how bad
We talk about his ass
As soon as he's out the door

Cool, he's in a good mood
Money is flowing and so is the food
Me and Wife in Law are good
Together we're always working on a
Way to get out of the hood

We break away and leave the Spoiler behind
Now he's not on anybody's mind
We can't be mad, he left this world
Never knowing what he did

We're grateful to him for bringing us together
Because we're still hanging in watching each others back
Vowing to be friends forever

Work All Your Life

Cynthia Young
April 29, 2012

Work, work, work, a necessary evil
I got bills to pay, I need to
Get up and hit the road every day

Save my money to buy what I need
Some day, I'll get myself a deed

Working and doing my very best, I can't complain
Pay days are good and
I'm living in a good neighborhood

One day soon, I'll realize my dreams
If I don't work too hard and run out of steam

Got to have money for a future day
Retirement sounds good and I'm own my way

Rum punch in hand, watching the sunset on
Another beautiful day, I'm on a white sandy beach
With warm Caribbean waters lapping around my feet

Man oh Man, this retirement life is sweet!

Stuff

Cynthia Young
February 17, 2014

We all have stuff we want to keep
We drag it from place to place like so many sheep

What does it matter all this stuff
After awhile it begins to look real rough

Your valuables are sold, they won't keep
Pictures, clothes or anything that's old
It only meant something to you in life

It seems in the end, nobody but you cared
About your stuff and it is discarded
Without a second thought
Leaving your stuff in a pile of dust

Siblings

Cynthia Young
May 10, 2012

Siblings getting together can be sweet or
Sour as soon as they meet

From the same Mother or not
They all have issues they want to come out

Argue and fight that's what siblings do
But be careful, outsiders 'cause they
Damn sure can turn on you

Interfere if you dare, so let me make you aware
They'll bond against you and you'll be nowhere

Hating, jealousy, rivalry and pride can divide siblings and
Make them take sides

Siblings will come together in time and
Iron out their differences or not

But you can count on one thing
There will always be one
That keeps stirring the damn pot

Complainer

Cynthia Young
August 02, 2012

We all know someone that complains all the time and
Never seems to be satisfied with their life

A Complainer
Just doesn't get it when it comes to
Your friendship

They complain
To you constantly until
It wears you thin
But you don't say anything
'Cuz you want to be a friend

Please! give it a rest, day in and
Day out, puts a strain on my
Nerves and makes me want to shout

They don't realize it depresses
You too and if they do
They don't care about you

You see its all about them, all the
Time, it's what's happening in their
World from the word hello

You won't get in another word
From then on out and you're holding your
Tongue to keep from bugging out

But friends stand by friends through
Thick and thin
Listening and consoling to the very end

The Bully

Cynthia Young
August 2012

The Bully is bold and can be very cold
Strutting like a peacock down the road

Always trying to do you one better
The Bully uses your ideas and
Never gives you any credit

The Bully says:
Oh, no you don't
You won't get ahead of me
I'll talk louder and shout
And won't let you get a word out

I'm always right, I'll just show you
You can't out do me no matter what
You do

I'll beat you down in the ground
And let you know I won another round

I'm the top dog here, you better believe
I got all the card tricks up my sleeve

I know it all, yes I do
And I can beat you any day
No matter what you try to do

Is this Bully tiring to you?
Well, you bet and there's something
You can do

Ignore the Bully and walk away
It takes two to tango any day
And
Without an audience
All that bluster and shout
Falls apart and peters out

Lover

Cynthia Young
August 02, 2012

A Lover is like no other
They can make your heart flutter
And melt you like butter

A Lover greets you with a warm
Gentle kiss and makes love
To you without being there
But
You can still feel his hand strokes
Running through your hair

A Lover touches you deep in your soul
And your mind and
Leaves memories of
The passion you have behind

Oh, a Lover gets deep down in your
Core and all you can think about
Is more, more, more!

Come to me Lover and do what you do
There is no one I'd rather be with than you

A Lover is smooth, sensual and slow
Moving with you to and fro

You both know exactly what to do
Love like this can blow your mind and
A Lover knows, when and how to make
You climb

Rock my world and let me know I'm the one
Call my name and yessssss, I'll be done

A Lover is someone you'll never forget and
You'll replay each moment you are together
From the day you met

Loving Me

Cynthia Young
August 02, 2012

Loving me is the first thing I do
Because I need to do this before
I can truly love you

Loving me gets cast to the side
For I am forever keeping you in mind

What is it with me, why can't I hold
On to my pride and stick to the things
I want way down deep inside

I have hopes and I have dreams
But I wind up letting someone
Talk me into getting caught
Up in their schemes

Starting over is hard to do
But I have to pick myself up and
Remember what to do
I need to love me, before I can love you

Giving of myself is who I am
It's what I know, it's what I yearn but learning to love me
Is my first life lesson to learn

Mojo

Cynthia Young
August 02, 2012

Your Mojo cast a spell on me, now
I know exactly where I want to be

The Mojo is strong and I'm in deep
I think about it so much, I can't even sleep
I've never been to heaven
Is this what it could be, like the Mojo
That sends shivers all over me?

I don't ever want these feelings
To become a thing of the past
So, please Baby, let's make this last

Soul Chicks

Cynthia Young
August 02, 2012

Soul Chicks have big wide hips
Beautiful, smooth brown skin and full pouty lips

Soul Chicks shimmy and shake to a beat and
Heads turn when they walk down the street

Always stylish, hair in the wind
Brown eyes sparkle with love and
There's a cleft in her chin

Can't miss that smile or her curves
Men want to speak but they lose their nerve

Soul Chick is cool, she'll talk to you
Bring a game that's proper and
She won't stop you

Come lame and she'll step on your game
And bring you to shame

Respect is what she demands and
There are plenty that want to take her hand
So they can become her man

Soul Chick is a mother, a lover and friend
She knows how to treat you and
Her loyalty is never a trend

When you meet a Soul Chick
You will know, because
Her class and grace is
The first thing that will show

I Don't Want To

Cynthia Young
August 02, 2012

Can you do this, will you do that
No, I don't want to

Words I don't often say, but need to
To learn to survive day to day

People are all over me, do this, do that
Can't you see, I don't have any time
Left for me
So,
No, I don't want to

Leave me alone, I just want to listen to
This song, take a long hot bath
Watch my favorite TV show and laugh

Pay this bill, go here, and go there
Sometimes I want to pull out my hair
Don't ask me again
Because, what?
I don't want to

I get it, you're needy and kind' a greedy
Hogging all my time, not leaving
Me space to have my peace of mind
I'll tell you again
And
Yes, I'm still your friend, momma and wife
But
I don't want to . . . .

Seriously, you need to get a life!

Tragedy Strikes

Cynthia Young
August 02, 2012

Tragedy struck one warm afternoon
While watching a film in a dim room

Lives were lost and many were hurt
There wasn't much to be done
Just pray that they capture the jerk

Miracles were born and love surrounds
those that survived the tragedy
that struck their town

Rapid water rose high
And swept lives away
A President did nothing that tragic day

Planes flew above and blew skyscrapers away
As I stood in my room
And watched on TV that fateful day

We don't know why, we don't know when
Tragedy like this will strike again

Keep prayer in your heart and
Know, that we have survived many
Times with bravery and grace

The United States of America
Is
And continues to be a great place!

Exclusive

Cynthia Young
August 03, 2012

You need to be a one woman man if
You want to be with me

'Cause a cheater brings the fire and
Ice right out of me

If I'm yours and you're mine
Love will be sweet

I'll love you the best from your
Head to your feet

With that understanding
We're good to go
Let's make love not war

With my straight talk, now
You know what you
Need to know

Stay exclusive to me
I'll do the same
And we won't have
Any shame in our game

I Need to Lose Weight

Cynthia Young
August 05, 2012

Here I am again looking in the mirror
At my double chins
I need to lose weight
And
No matter how hard I try
It still lingers all over my thighs

Don't eat this, don't eat that
I'm so hungry right now
I could eat my hat

Oh boy, I think I'll try
Exercise, nope that didn't
Work either by the look
Of my thighs

What's a girl to do
When the weight
Just hangs on all over you

Skinny girls I hate to say
I used to be one of you
Back in the day

Age and stress have put me to a test
That I failed miserably
I just eat my way
Through all the ice cream and cake
I see

Looking at the results of that binge
Make me want to jump in the lake

I don't want to be
This greasy grease
The fat is hanging all over my knees

I need to lose weight, so I'll try again!
I've got to get rid of my fat thighs
And
Double chins!

Beauty Shop

Cynthia Young
August 05, 2012

Dedicated to Winnye, Kim, Winsome and Gerri

Beauty Shops
Give us hair styles galore,
Short, long, braided and weaved
Hats off to our Hair Stylist
Who give us any style we can conceive

Good conversation and laughs galore, this is
Where girlfriends get hooked up
To go to a show

Nails and feet are groomed to the nines
Buffed and polished
With pretty colors and designs of the time

Hair piled high, or hanging down low
Girlfriends leave the salon
With a smile on their face

All dressed up with your hair in place
Make up on all over your face
Now that you're all fluffed and puffed

There's nothing left to do
But hit the clubs
So all the men can admire you!

Red Light Party

Cynthia Young
August 04, 2012

Dedicated to Le Roy, Belinda, Joan, Marcus, Billy, Bruce and Grant

It's 1962 the music is flowing
Dancers under the glowing red lights
Turn my mother's basement into
A party tonight

We're doing it big!
We've got homemade punch and potato chips
Everyone in our block is at this gig

Oh no! Here she comes, we're not supposed
To have those red lights on
If she catches us, it will ruin our night

Somebody put the white lights in, they did it
So fast it would make your head spin

Mom's finally gone, now we can turn
The red lights back on

We're just mischievous teens
Doing our thing
Having lots of good clean fun

The forbidden
Red lights make our night and
Our red light party is out of sight!

Childhood Friends

Cynthia Young
August 02, 2012

Dedicated to Le Roy, Belinda, Joan, Marcus, Billy, Bruce and Grant

We met in 1958
I was new to the neighborhood
Boys and girls gathered around
And I felt welcomed and good

We became a tight knit group
Holding each others secrets
Never telling a soul

We worked out our problems
Together, even 'til this day
As we've grown old

We had our code of silence
That's the way we rolled

We had much fun and troubles too
Seeing our friends go off to the Viet Nam war

Even though we scattered across the states
We still come together no matter what
Our friendships still goes deep and strong
I can't imagine any of us alone

Finally, as grown ups
Sitting around the dining room table
We decided to tell Mom about our fables

We stuck together as childhood friends
And
Here we are today, doing the same thing

Much love and devotion to each one of you
Because I know your hearts
I know you feel the same way about me too

My Daddy

Cynthia Young
August 04, 2012

Dedicated to my father

My Daddy is the first man I ever loved
There was nothing and no one
That stood above

He is handsome and smart and
Plays soulful songs on his Saxophone

My Daddy is bad with a gun
He can hit anything
Moving under this sun

His sharp tongue cuts to the quick
There have been many days
I had to give my wounds a lick

I missed him when he left
I cried and just wanted to die
I couldn't imagine him not being with me

I stood on the back porch and watched as he
Drove away in the Ford that awful day

Did I do something to make him flee?
I screamed, please Daddy, don't leave me!

Years have passed and I am older now
I realize that he had to go
It wasn't about me, that much I know

Daddy
Thank you for your
Support when I needed it

You stepped up and made things right
And I love you Daddy, with all of my might

Red Satin Dress

Cynthia Young
August 04, 2012

Dedicated to my mother

It was 1955 and I could only see through
Wide innocent eyes

Brown sugar skin and pouty red lips
That matched her Red Satin Dress

Hair curled to perfection, I stare
At her from the doorway and
Watch her as she sways away

Mother's going dancing tonight
At The Flame Show Bar
That's all the rage these days

Rhinestones glitter around her neck
And in her ears
She is to me a beautiful sight

She'll never be more beautiful to me
Than she is this very night

President Obama

Cynthia Young
August 04, 2012

President Obama,
The first of our race
Took a powerful position
With style and grace

He has stood up to all his
Haters and continues
To
Win over the human race

Yes, the haters disrespect
Him by saying rude things
We all expected that to
Be the routine

His swagger is smooth
He's educated and cool
Pretty wife by his side
He is a leader
That gives us pride

Much love is what we have
For a role model that's
Great, he's given our young
Men something to contemplate

He holds his head high
And
Walks like the man he is,
always looking to the sky

He is the one,
That is heaven sent
God bless our President!

Seventh Child

Cynthia Young
August 07, 2012

Dedicated to my mother

She was the seventh child of eight and
God took her home on the seventh day

She had her way, she wanted to stay
Where she was born until her last day

She had brown sugar skin
That she never neglected to tend

A gap graced her smile and she
Would invite you to stay awhile
Have some good cookin' play some music and dance

The kids in her block took no chance being late to the table
Where she amused and awed us with her fables

She kept us in check all our growing years, but
She always hugged and kissed away our fears

We loved her until
She left here on the seventh day
Just as she wanted, she did it her way

Courage!

Cynthia Young
October 01, 2012

Courage! is what I need to face my challenges
And
Meet my needs

Not always there, I pull from deep within
To summon my courage from my
Feet to my chin

Instilled with courage I approach each day
Standing up to whatever may come my way
Courage! Is what I have and it lives within me

Courage! To fight a good fight
Courage! To set things right
I keep my head up and face my plight
Chasing my fears off into the night

Trust Me

Cynthia Young
October 03, 2012

Girl, do you believe . . . .
Another man has come into my life
Uttering Baby trust me

He talked a good game
And
All during sex he hollered my name
But, lo and behold
His ulterior motives start to show

I'll have the last laugh because
Little does he know, I have
Seen his game, 'cause I've
Been through it before

His bags are packed and he's headed
Out the door, 'cause
Just saying "trust me" doesn't
Cut it any more!

Lessons Learned

Cynthia Young
September 28, 2012

Years come and years go
Only to give me what I know

Lessons learned
Along the way, have kept me
Straight until this very day
Some were good and some were bad
None the less I got my share

I climbed my peaks and enjoyed the sights
And
Endured the valleys
As a part of life

My lessons learned have taught me well
I passed my teachings
To those I know
To save them from pitfalls
And
To help them grow

You may not
Understand the lesson at hand
But trust and believe
It may be revealed over time
As life continues to move down the line

Failure Is Not an Option

Cynthia Young
October 03, 2012

Smooth talking, easy going, you believe
He is truly the one
He's the head of the house
He says he's in control

Things happen to well laid plans when you entrust
Your future to a competitive, jealous, spoiled, egotistical man

Things come to light in the middle of the night
Secrets are revealed and questions
Are abound, damn this
Relationship is going down

Now you have to take matters into your hands,
To pull up out of a failed plan
Your money is gone
And it's another sad song

You're angry and frustrated
How could this happen
He couldn't handle
The reins after all his lip flappin'

It's late in life to be dealing with this strife
Failure is not an option at this stage of life
Pick yourself up by your boot straps
Once again,
Shake it off and
Swear off men

Dark Corners

Cynthia Young
December 02, 2012

I can't seem to leave the dark corners of my mind
I have been there since my mom died and I'm having a hard time
Leaving them behind is not happening too fast

I'm told that they won't last
I see happy and I see sad, I have laughter and I feel mad
In the dark corners of my mind

I want to leave and I will, I know
I hear my mom whispering, Baby I'm okay go on and
Leave me, its time for you to go

The dark corners will have light one day,
And I will walk away with insight,
The darkness in the corners of my mind will take flight
And leave me standing in the sunshine's bright light

Broken Moon

Cynthia Young
September 14, 2012

A Broken Moon
In
Midnight skies brings
Salty tears to my eyes
It reflects the way I feel

My head and heart still reel
From a heavy loss that rocked
My world

My mother went to sleep
And
Quietly left this world
Leaving behind her little girl

A Broken Moon comes and goes
Like my salty tears that
Ebb and flow

Perhaps one day soon
I'll look differently
At the
Broken Moon,
But not just yet,
It's still too soon

Sapphires and Pearls

Cynthia Young
February 23, 2013

Dedicated to my mother and daughter

Sapphires and Pearls
Represent both my
Very best girls

I'm in the middle of my
mom and my baby
I definitely have love
For them and that's
Without maybe

I would do anything
In this world
For my Sapphires and Pearls

Love and honor is easy
To give
Mom and Daughter are the
reasons I live

Sapphires and Pearls
There is nothing too good
For my girls
One is gone but her
Memory lives on

My baby girl
Brings me laughter and light
And
She always brightens my world

Step to the Side

Cynthia Young
May 02, 2013

When life throws you out of stride
Take a step to the side

Stand there quietly
Take a deep breath, relax
And close your eyes

Never question why it's your turn to take a step to the side
And don't be tempted to go backwards because of pride

One door closes but God makes other ways
Until then, just step to the side

And
Look forward to better days

Belly Pop and Bootie Drop

Cynthia Young
June 02, 2013

I stood in the mirror and what did I see
My belly popped out and my bootie
Dropped behind my knees

My friends all agree the belly pop and the
Bootie drop doesn't just apply to me

Don't you see, youngsters today already look like
Me. Sagging boobs, butts and chins
Make me think, they won't make it
To the end

If they look like that now, what will
They look like at my age
When they've been carrying
The belly pop and bootie drop
Since they were babes

If you don't suck it up and
Tuck it in now, you won't make
It to a ripe old golden age
Wake up youngsters and take
Care of yourselves, 'cause getting
Old really will be hell

Slave to the Weave

Cynthia Young
October 21, 2012

So many of us are slaves to the weave
It has a grip on our vanity so tough
It will drop you to your knees

I won't give up my weave, because I love the look
Hair flowing and blowing shaking my head
Back and forth so hard, I gave myself a crook

I'm a slave to the weave there is no doubt!
If I can't get my hair done, I'm ready to pout!

Got' a keep good cash flow 'cause good weave
Ain't cheap. I need to look good from my head
To my feet

I'll be a slave, there's no shame in my game
I own my weave, like I own my name

Fluid Hips

Cynthia Young
March 13, 2013

Fluid hips can make a man lick his lips
She sways and gyrates back and forth, leaving
Him swooning as she leaves the dance floor
The crowd yelled to come back and give them more

He speaks slick words to get her alone
As he walks with her arm and arm
On her way home

She knows his kind, she's too smart to
Let him get in her mind

She smiled at him as she slipped away
As he looked at her with longing in his eyes
He tried to conceal the swelling that
Crept between his thighs

Her fluid hips, were tempting
He wanted to fill her with his seed
But he'd have to keep licking his lips
With his hand in his pocket dreaming
About doing the deed

The Blame Game

Cynthia Young
June 5, 2013

The blame game never seems to end
It's a never ending loop that tears
Through family and friends

I can't get a word in to speak my piece
You can't let go of an image in
Your head, of a white picket fence
And Ol' Saint Nick kissing
you good night in bed

You blame me for your troubles now
And everything in between, but
You never say all the good things I
Did to keep you happy
By any means

Blame, blame, blame
What a shame I can't get you to see
That you had better than most kids
With a mother worse than you call me
I'm not perfect, I never claimed to be
At some point, just be you
And let me be me

Your troubles are your own, you made
That bed you're in, all I tried to do is
Keep you safe and be your mother and a friend

No mater what I say, or what I do
You keep making everything
All the time just about you

Listen sometimes and maybe you
Will see, that I did the best I could
You're a mother and you're about to learn
How hard it is
'Cuz Baby, now it's your turn

Processed Hair

Cynthia Young
June 5, 2013

Oooh wee, do you smell that awful odor
Floating through the air
That's the smell of processed hair

Lye and chemicals, made a brother sweat
But keeping his "do" looking good
Was what he needed
To go out and catch

Every chocolate city had the prime barber shop
That kept the pimps and players
Coming in and out

Lenny was the man that had the slight of hand
He fried, dyed and laid that hair to the side
He kept his shop booming
Hogs lined up on 12th street
Kept the girls looming

A players and pimps paradise, the
Barber shop was the place to be
He left with his processed hair
As shiny as it could be

In the newest Cadillac and a woman on
His arm, his shiny processed hair
Was the latest craze in town

Trickery

Cynthia Young
June 5, 2013

I see you like playing tricks
Collaborating with your friends
Trying to be slick

Instead of that, try the truth
I see through your trickery
And you don't even know
I had your number
When you walked through
The door

Believe me it's all good, if you don't
Want to be around, just be honest
And there will be less for me to clown

You're not slick enough to pull one
Over on me,
I've been in this world
A lot longer than you
And I know all the trickery
That you could attempt to do

Stay true to yourself, don't
Try to fool me
I don't care one way or
the other
Especially since I set you free!
Now, you don't have to
Worry about lying to me

Robbed

Cynthia Young
June 10, 2013

For those of us who have jobs
It's hard to see ourselves being robbed
Thieves come on you day or night
The street lights are out so
You have to decide whether it's
Best to fight or take flight

Where are the police? Nowhere these days
Sitting in the precinct from budget cuts
And Mayor's doing nothing but
Sitting on their butts

Robbers have a job too and that's to
Take what you have earned away from you

We're being robbed, thieves love
Taking your stuff, but citizens are fighting back
We've been through hell and we've had enough!

Cougar

Cynthia Young
September 01, 2013

I am a Cougar, oh yes I am
I love a strong, intelligent young man
I know what they like
And
I am hot to trot
Seeing things their way
I know how to be out of the box

Cougars are wise and in demand
We keep things together
And don't really need a man

Young men love us and we know why
We have lived through the silliness
And dreams in the sky

My body is tight, sex is off the hook
We don't have to worry about making babies, so
Twist me this way and that way
It's all very good

Young men love us
'cuz we know the ropes
And
We know how to help them
Achieve their hopes

Gay Pride

Cynthia Young
September 01, 2013

We have overcome
Our Gay and Lesbian pride
Is number one

Now we can marry and raise a family too
It's been a long time coming
And we feel brand new

Love is blind and we know
We are judged, but it
Doesn't stop who I choose to love

Equal rights for us is what we fought for
Now we have our foot in the door
And we won't stop fighting
To achieve even more

The Borrower

Cynthia Young
September 01, 2013

You borrowed my money and my stuff
Now you have the nerve to be mad at me
'Cuz I called to ask about it
You're hollering like a crazed banshee

You must not watch Judge Mathis on TV
I have a right to call and see
When you'll get my money
Back to me

Sister, Brother, friend that you are, how dare you be rude
When all I did was try to help you
Our relationship just took a great big shift
I loaned you my money it was not a gift

I'll tell you one thing and you can
Take this to the bank
I'm not the one to mess with
So don't jack with me
You'll never get another dime
Just try and you'll see

A Good Man

Cynthia Young
September 01, 2013

Men, can't live with 'em
Can't live without 'em

Young and fine, old and wise
Men come in every shape color
And size

Bald or afro I love a man
Who's neat and clean
Pretty white teeth
With shoes shined to a tee

Sagging and bagging not for me
That's the new school way
Give me a brother who's style
Is an updated look from back in the day

Tall or short, personality abound
A sense of humor too
A job and money in the bank
Keeps him from being stank

Lord, give me a good man who
Loves me and has his feet
planted firmly on the ground
Please send him soon, 'cuz my clock is ticking
And we need to be getting down

Sons and Daughters

Cynthia Young
September 01, 2013

Son's and daughter's take heed
You are a product from our seed
You're the new generation
To take over this great nation

We've laid the ground work but
There is still much to do
To save this country and the world
From prejudice, slavery and injustice too

Hold your head up and step to the plate
We know you can be great, be responsible
It's never too late

Young men, pick up your pants
How in the world can you even dance
Young ladies, classy is the impression
You want to leave, not slutty
Wearing a whacked weave

Facebook, Twitter and the like
Be careful what you post there
It can be seen by anyone, anywhere

Keep your heads on straight and make
Us proud, you are the future
We'll say it loud
You are the future, make us proud!

Warriors

Cynthia Young
September 01, 2013

Our men and women go off to war
I thank you for your service
From shore to shore
And
All over this world
Leaving behind a guy or girl

With every breath in my body,
I reach out and touch your pain
I hail you all with love
Because of you and the greatest sacrifice you
Can give, your life is not in vain

.

Life and freedom, the right to vote
Free speech is everywhere in our streets

I pray that one day
The whole world will see the beautiful white dove
Touching every shore with peace and love

Cookie Jar

Cynthia Young
June 27, 2013

Momma had a cookie jar
She filled with cookies
We could smell from afar

Warm and gooey, soft and chewy
We never missed a day
Putting our hands in the cookie jar
Before we went out to play

Momma's cookie jar is more than fifty years old
And is still in tact as a matter of fact

We'll never forget the memories that cookie jar
Brings back

Now, that Momma is gone the cookie jar sits empty and alone
Covered in a layer of dust like lace
Still on top of the fridge in its hallowed place

Use Me

Cynthia Young
September 22, 2013

I don't mind helping you, I never did
But you are about to make me
Blow my lid

I don't mind that you use me
That's perfectly fine
Just don't try and
Abuse me or I will
Lose my mind

You take my kindness for weakness
Stop! Don't argue with me
Yes! You do!
I'm always the one
Giving to you

Use me, don't abuse me
Now that's something
I won't allow you to do

Keep messing with me
If you want to and
I will show you
That'll be the last
Thing you do

Can't Say No

Cynthia Young
September 22, 2013

You love to help whenever you can, lots of people
Are calling and you are always in demand
At first being the center of attention
Was fun, you loved basking in those rays of sun

Now, you get
Calls for this and that
You don't say no, but you want to
You can't say no to the Teacher
You won't say no to the Preacher
Because you don't really want to

Your ego is in the way, you like the
Attention they give you every day
Learn to say no, and they will
Stop knocking on your door

Let the phone ring and pass up the chance
To handle a project that
Takes up all your time

Don't complain when you can't
Sit down and enjoy
A glass of wine,
But realize that your ego
Has got to stop feeding the flow

People will run a good thing in the ground
If you don't stand up for yourself
And just say no!
You'll continue to be on their merry-go-round

Midnight and Moonlight

Cynthia Young
May 27, 2013

Midnight and Moonlight
One dark and one light
Met in the neighborhood
In the bright summer sunlight

Midnight and Moonlight
Have been friends from
First sight, having
Each other's back through thick and thin
Through Viet Nam's horrors
And slick talking men

Their friendship prevails
Over years of laughter,
Sorrow and childhood tales

Nothing can mar the
Love years of friendship begets
Midnight and Moonlight look forward to fifty
More years with no regrets

The Turn Around

Cynthia Young
September 25, 2013

It's been months since you shut me out
I never thought you would carry
Your threats out

You're stressed and I can see that
All your hateful words and actions are
Spewing out towards me

Today, I heard your voice and the
Humility is evident, you've
Been through a lot
And I'm sorry
Coming from you means so much

I love you and always will
I've told you many times
How I feel, I'm so
Happy you're back in my life
Let's move forward
One day at a time
And
Make a fresh start to
Cleanse our hearts and minds

Food Stamps

Cynthia Young
September 30, 2013

I've never used food stamps before
Now they are a necessity
I can't live without any more

Just trying to make ends meet
My worker cut my food stamps and it
Will be hard to buy enough food to eat

These days, every little bit helps
Big or small
I'm going to give my worker another call
I hope she will hear my plea
'Cuz 25 dollars a month in food stamps
Is barely enough to feed me

.

I'm Free!

Cynthia Young
September 30, 2013

He held me back and controlled my every move
I could never get comfortable in my own groove

He was controlling, never consoling and he
Couldn't stand for me to be out of his sight
He called it love, but it still didn't feel right

No one could look at me, if they did
He wanted to fight
One day, I walked away and never
Looked back, I was fed up
And I had enough

I'm free to be me
And that's what matters
Don't you see

I will never let another person
Have that kind of control over me
I woke up! And now I'm Free!

Compromise

Cynthia Young
September 30, 2013

Day in and day out all over the world
Sacrifices are made through compromise

Man, woman, boy or girl,
Presidents, Pontiffs
Husbands and wives
Compromise to save relationships
And lives

Don't be afraid to give a little
It doesn't make you lose
But rather you can win,
To know that through compromise
You gave something
But didn't give all the way in

1974

Cynthia Young
September 30, 2013

Dedicated to Tanya and Donny

Three friends left Detroit in two cars and a van
To seek a new life in a different land

California here we come
Across the Painted Desert
Seeing Joshua trees for
The very first time
Down from the mountain peak
We descended into smog filled skies

No matter, the sun was bright and hot
That November day,
We drove into LA and found our way
Down famous streets we saw on TV

Excitement abound, we scoured the town
We rode the Hollywood Strip
And saw the Brown Derby too
This is definitely where we
Wanted to settle down

Thirty-eight years later, its been a good life
The ocean and snow capped mountains
Malibu, Beverly Hills, Marina del Rey
There is still so much to see
I love California, its been good to me
And
It's still the only place I want to be

Throwing Shade

Cynthia Young
April 15, 2014

This shade is not the kind you find standing under a tree
No, this shade is what you're trying to throw
All over me

Your shade won't cover my light
I know who I am
That's why I can stand upright

I'm breaking through your shade
With my words and my deeds

So back up and stop trying to
Put on a show for everyone
To see

You definitely aren't smart
Enough to throw shade that I won't see

Because you are in no way
Smart enough to play in my league!

Broke Down

Cynthia Young
September 30, 2013

You've been working hard
All your life caring for others
Beating back heartache and strife

Down times have gotten better
It's time for you to relax
Now that you have, you're all broke down

What! It's not suppose to be like this
It's time for me to have
Joy and happiness

But, the body begs to differ
In and out of doctor's appointments
What's that he's saying?
Something's wrong with my liver!
Oh no, it can't be, breaking down
Can't be my fate, get this body moving
It's never too late!

Touch Me

Cynthia Young
October 01, 2013

Touch me, I know you want to
Touch me, I want you to
Slide your hand down
And touch the crown

Touch me, it's what you've been waiting for
I want you to touch deep down in the groove
Don't worry, I won't move

Sensual and hot, your breath on me makes
Me tingle and I visualize the motion of the sea
Rocking deep down inside of me

Your touch is velvet, I love it so
Don't stop stroking me, 'til I say
You can go . . . . come on and touch me

Homeless

Cynthia Young
October 03, 2013

I once had a house, car and money, just like you
You look at me withered, tattered and torn
Looking very forlorn

You wonder what happened to me
Why am I living on the street with
A shopping cart under a tree

Was I into drugs and irresponsible
I had a job and money in the bank
The market took a turn, my baby got sick
I lost my job and I got burned

Overwhelmed with too many bills to pay
I had no teckkie skills that are needed today
Don't pity me
I want to live a better life and
Remove myself from this awful scary, smelly
Dirty street life

Don't judge too harshly, you could come to be me
Sitting with a shopping cart under a tree

Stashed Away

Cynthia Young
October 03, 2013

I'm old and gray, I don't remember too well
I'm stricken with ailments
My family argues about what to do with me

Nobody wants to give up their life
Work, children and other demands is what's
Causing them to throw up their hands

Stash me away in a home
I understand
That's where I'll be until I'm dead and gone

Stash me away and don't feel guilty
I'm telling you now
I understand
I'll love you just the same

Live your life, I have lived mine
And now it's your turn to shine
Stash me away, I'll be okay
I know the end is near and
I'm looking forward to a better day

Dangerous Curves

Cynthia Young
October 20, 2013

Dangerous curves from head to toe
This girl was fabulous when she walked out the door

Men wanted her to be their wife
Showered her with
Mink coats and diamond rings
These are just a few of the gifts they bring

They look and they wonder what it would be like
To ride her dangerous curves all through the night

Ahh, those curves make men and women swoon
With thoughts that make them howl
Like a wolf at the moon

She walks with her head held high
Never seeming to notice the commotion she caused

She walks with purpose and grace
Then suddenly turns and nods to her admirers
With a beautiful smile on her face

Get Some Business of Your Own

Cynthia Young
October 20, 2013

The break up was fresh, tears flowed and flowed
Then anger set in and you had to talk with your girls
Rage and revenge set in, it was all you could think of

But wise and cool your best friend took you to school
She said girl don't you fret, dry those tears
You've got a lot going for you, don't
Worry about what he's doing
Get some business of your own
And watch how fast his ass wants to come back home

Stop watching and calling and crying the blues
Get some business of your own
And he'll be the one pursuing you

Don't have any regrets, things happen for a reason
Men come and go for a lifetime or a season
If he's meant for you, he'll come back
And straighten up his act

Meanwhile, get some business of your own
And there is no doubt he'll drop that other woman
When he finds out that the grass wasn't greener like he thought

The Only Son

Cynthia Young
October 20, 2013

My dad is sick and wants to go, he hurts
Every day I see him so I know

He's given up hope for me
His only son, I can't tell him
All the things I've done

He wanted a better life for me, his only son
I know the path I took is not the right one

I struggle now to make it right
I don't want him to go,
I want him to see, I can be a better man
But I fear it's too little too late

I'm sorry Dad, I let you down
And that is my cross to bear
I pray you'll forgive me
Before you take your last breath
Or I will never get over your death

Booty Call

Cynthia Young
October 20, 2013

The phone rings late at night
A smile crosses your face
Suddenly there's a knock at the door
Black lingerie and chilled wine glasses
Set the scene

The candles are glowing, you and your guy
Are flowing, the sex is wild that's putting it mild

Satisfied and glowing, in the back of your mind
You know this feeling won't last,
'Cuz he's getting dressed on
His way out, now that he's smacked that ass

Hustler

Cynthia Young
October 21, 2013

Hustling in the streets
Money is tight
Got' a do what it takes
To make things right

Up late at night
Playing casino slots
Lotto tickets are all over the house

Trying to hustle up on the rent
Car note and bill money
Man, I'm taking heat from my Honey

Hustling ain't the same as it was
Back in the day
Now, I need to find a
Different way

My heart ain't big as a mustard seed
Stealing copper, robbing in the streets
Definitely not my cup of tea, because
Jail is definitely, not somewhere I'm trying to be

Faded

Cynthia Young
October 26, 2013

In and out, in and out
Sometimes I can't seem to figure out
Where I am, who I am, or even what I'm doing

Who are you? I don't know
I can't remember how to put my clothes on

In and out, in and out
What's happening to me, I'm not sure
My brains in a fog, it's fading away
I'm losing my memories
From the present and back in the day

They say Alzheimer's is what's wrong with me
My children worry all the time that
I'll walk away to the other side of town

Faded away, the memories are gone
I can't remember the words
To my favorite love song

It's the fate that God chose for me
I'm locked inside my mind and can't get out
No one knows what I'm talking about

I'll fade away one day at a time
Don't be sad, I lived a good life
Love me the way I am until I'm gone
Then remember me by
Playing all my favorite songs

Alone

Cynthia Young
January 31, 2014

She sits alone in her room wondering if
She'll ever escape her gloom

What's going to happen to her now
That she's sickly alone and grey

Who will help her, will she die alone
That is the question now that no one ever phones

She knows she ran everyone away
She didn't want their help then
But this is another day

To proud to reach out
She sits in her room wondering
If she'll ever escape her gloom

Did she live her life right? Is this how karma
Is making things right?

She sadly contemplates her fate
And wonders when her maker will
Choose her date

Life Happens in Rhyme

Cynthia Young
January 31, 2014

In my mind life happens in rhyme
All the time, day by day
I hear myself say, here's
Another chance to find romance, hear a bird
Sing or do more things

Life happens in rhyme
Everywhere I look, I want to see joy
A father walking with his baby boy
I want to hear laughter abound
Not people running from bombs
In every town

A soundtrack plays in my head to
All the events that
Have lead to the life I have now
Because of God's blessings
I humbly give thanks and take a bow

In my mind, life happens in rhyme

My Love

Cynthia Young
January 31, 2014

Dedicated to my husband

With his big brown eyes, smooth chocolate skin
A killer smile that drives me wild,
Rich baritone voice that makes
Me flutter inside
He stole my heart and didn't give it back

He gave me flowers, cars and pretty things
The romance was awesome
Even without those things

Swaying to the grooves of
Sade and Tina Marie
He whispered beautiful words to me

We tied the knot, jumped the broom
He was such a handsome groom

We laugh and play together
Pray and fuss together
Love and praise each other

He knows how to take charge
Leading the way down
Our path in life

He is the man I always dreamed about
He makes me proud to be his wife

Cexy

Cynthia Young
February 01, 2014

Her name is Cexy
Big pretty legs, bow hips and Revlon red lips
I fell to the side to peep her
Sexy stride

Sexing her was on my mind
How would it feel deep in her well
Climbing to new heights I'd never known
Hickeys on my neck never to be shown

Sex with her was amazing, rubbing
Stroking, damn near choking
She made me blast, but not too fast

Sex with her makes me scream
But she didn't even notice me
As she walked away and out of my dream

Invisible

Cynthia Young
February 01, 2014

Old people need to be invisible these days
The youngsters don't want us to get
In their way

There's no respect for the elders like it used to be
They cuss and holler and call you dude
Like I'm they're friend,
I never thought things would
Come to this end

Gray haired people have to hurry home before the
Street lights come on,
These days it's a shame we can't feel safe any place

I wish I was invisible when I see one coming
'cuz I never know if it's a gun I'll be facing
Robbing, killing it's just too much
I'm too scared these days to go out and have lunch

Using canes, walkers, wheelchairs too, you'd better not
Get in the way of the youngsters these days
Rude and obnoxious is how they roll
With no honor and respect for
Those that are old

She Likes to Ride

Cynthia Young
February 02, 2014

She likes to ride in a fast car on 22's
Chrome fangs flash and lash out as
She comes your way and
She's dressed to the nines in her bad ass shoes

She loves her whip and shows it off
Men, women and children stop and stare
She's the one that likes to take on a dare

The girl's got fever for speed
Never one to back down
She burns rubber to feed her need

She likes to ride, but fast cars aside
Her man is the lucky one when
She feels that way
He'll be the one having a very groovy day

People are Crazy These Days

Cynthia Young
February 02, 2014

Road rage, shoot outs, robbing and killing
Back in the day, people use to be home chillin'

Today it's different, there's no courtesy these days
Just the bump of a shoulder can set it off
And the next thing you know
You're on the six o'clock news
Wondering what happened and giving your views

Three hundred snakes in the house, everywhere you
Looked there was a mouse, what was he thinking
The smell was horrific, now his dumb ass is sitting in jail

Singer gone wild, he's still nothing but a child
He's on the wrong path, but all he does is laugh
He won't be laughing if he goes to jail
And has to sing to a mop and pail

Little black Girl Scout selling cookies door to door
Was greeted by a white man who put a shotgun in her face
When he opened the door, he didn't see cookies
All he saw was her race

The Comedian

Cynthia Young
February 02, 2014

The Comedian, started thoughts swirling in my head
That changed my life
He told me to dream big
Keep your eye on the prize and it's your
Dreams that you'll realize

He painted a picture that I could see clearly
I wanted to pursue these things in my head dearly

Off to LA I went, looking for a way to vent
Joy, happiness and wonder abound
I decided to stay and live in this town

The Comedian was fun, we had a ball
From Detroit to LA
We partied and danced in every disco hall

He treated me like a queen and I was
Fortunate to never see him act mean
I'll never forget the funny man
He'll always have a place in my heart

Now, the Comedian is no longer here
I pray that he found the peace he longed for
And that God met him at heaven's door

Under the Bus

Cynthia Young
February 02, 2014

I know, you know someone you've tried to protect
Going the distance to stick out your neck
Only to find that when the going got rough
They caved in and gave you up

Now, you're in the forefront trying to keep down the fuss
While trying to get from under the bus

It's never good when you're under the bus
Friends, family, coworkers alike
No one steps up during the real fight

You're the one that's getting the side eye, wondering
How it is the bus landed on you, hopefully you have
Learned a lesson and now you know what not to do

Letting Go

Cynthia Young
February 09, 2014

The city was beautiful when I was a child
Now it is hateful, scary and people are on the wild

Stealing every chance they get, won't let you
Have the things you worked hard for
You wake up in the morning
And find your car stolen when you walk out the door

Abandoned houses run the neighborhood down
I can't keep my mother's house
'cuz the tenant's won't stick around

I wanted to keep the legacy she left for me
But circumstances are different these days
I have to let go, sell it and move away

Selling all her things, leaving nothing behind
Makes me feel like I'm losing my mind
The past is truly behind me, my future
And the unknown await me

This evolution was inevitable, I feel I've
Lost what she worked so hard for
There's nothing left here, but heartache and stress
I hope she knows I did my best

Cherish

Cynthia Young
February 09, 2014

Cherish means to hold dear, to love and never fear
A Mother should be treated this way

Some Mother's never know this feeling, they
Never nurtured their own and didn't know
How to make a house a home

Some Mother's were born to care
And never let wrong doing touch
Their baby's hair

All in all a Mother's love is what we
Want and need and we are blessed
If we are chosen by one
From above

Cherish the Mother you have while
She is still here and you'll never regret doing so
For a good Mother's love will follow
Wherever you go

Other People's Money

Cynthia Young
April 17, 2014

There you go again, talking about
What other people have
The way you try and disguise
Your contempt makes me want to laugh

You got mad because they didn't
Help you out and that's what
Your attitude is really all about

You count their money, when you hear them say
"I went to the nail shop and I got my hair done today
I bought cute shoes and a new dress too"

You can't be happy for someone else
Criticizing all they do, just because
It doesn't suit you

Who are you to say, how someone spends their pay
Stop counting other people's money, that's really not cool
Take it from me; you're making yourself sound like a damn fool

Sagging Pants

Cynthia Young
February 16, 2014

Pants baggy and sagging, running from the po po
Hiding behind garbage cans, hoping and praying
I can out run the man

My pants are falling down and so am I
The man is hooking me up, I'm on
My way to the can
All because of my sagging pants

My momma said this would happen to me
She wanted me to be all I can be
Now I'm headed to a cell
I feel like I'm in hell
All because of my sagging pants

Showing my under wear and the crack of my ass
Now, I'm running from some muscle bound broth' a
Lord help me, where is my mother

Trying to look like something I'm not
Don't worry Momma, I'm not going
To jail to rot

No more running from the man
I'm pulling up my sagging pants
These streets are too mean for me
I'm ready to be all I can be

Velvet Lips

Cynthia Young
March 03, 2014

Velvet Lips, soft and pink loves him
In all of his glory, so I'll keep the
Secret, and I won't go deep
Into his story

Velvet Lips, soft and pink
Makes him stop to think
How will he kiss those lips to
Bring his juices to their tip

Velvet Lips, soft and pink, quivers and
Sighs deep down inside, bringing great joy and
Tears to a grown man's eyes

He strokes those Velvet Lips, softly and
Kisses them often and those images are
Fresh in his head when he wakes
Up feeling lucky that she is in his bed

Brother on the Rise

Cynthia Young
March 05, 2014

I met a young brother who cut hair
He had a dream that he pulled from the air
He made it a reality and opened
His own shop, he beams with pride
His future looks bright
He is a brother on the rise

A young man with goals and drive
Makes me proud and hopeful
To see there are still young
Black men that seek more
Than running the streets
Looking to rob a store

A young brother with
His eyes on the prize
Is a brother on the rise

Legacy

Cynthia Young
August 02, 2012

I want to leave a legacy behind
And
Tell the story I acquired over time

A story that can only be mine
Is my legacy to leave behind

I leave memories of my past, for my
Daughter to see
And
I pray she will be proud of me

I leave a trail of love for my husband
Who stuck with me

I leave love letters for my mom and dad

I leave laughter and joy for my true friends
Who loved and supported me through thick and thin

This book is my legacy for all to know
I lived life to the fullest and I want
To show, that it wasn't for nothing
And
I will live on
In my rhymes and books
To a back drop of my
Favorite songs

About the Author

Photograph by Darryl Young
Hairstyle by Kim Best

Cynthia Young was born and raised in Detroit, Michigan. She graduated from Northwestern High School and later moved to California in 1974, where she resides today with her husband.

"Memoirs of a Caregiver" is her first literary work. In it she shares her experiences as a caregiver over the past twelve years for four family members—all of them stricken with Alzheimer's disease.

"Cynthology" is Young's second book. She expresses her view of life through her collection of unedited rhymes that she describes as short stories. There are more than one hundred rhymes, covering subjects from back in the day, current events, relationships, sorrow, sex, love and more, find your favorite(s) and enjoy!